# COGNITIVE BEHAVIORAL THERAPY

21 Most Effective Tips and Tricks on Retraining Your Brain and Overcoming Depression, Anxiety and Phobias

# Table of Contents

# INTRODUCTION

I want to thank you and congratulate you for purchasing the book, "Cognitive Behavioral Therapy: 21 Most Effective Tips and Tricks on Retraining Your Brain and Overcoming Depression, Anxiety and Phobias".

This book contains proven steps and strategies on how to rewire or retrain your brain in order to change how you see and feel certain difficulties that happen in your life. In effect, it can also help treat different issues such as: phobias, anxiety, and even depression.

This book gives you a brief overview of cognitive behavioral therapy and how it can help you control your thoughts and actions. It also gives you useful information about rewiring or retraining your brain to unlearn unhealthy thought patterns.

Thank you and I hope you enjoy it!

# Your Free Gift

As a way of saying thanks for your purchase, I wanted to offer you a free bonus E-book called *"How to Talk to Anyone: 50 Best Tips and Tricks to Build Instant Rapport"*.

Within this comprehensive guide, you will find information on:

- How to make a killer first impression

- Tips on becoming a great listener

- Using the FORM method for asking good questions

- Developing a great body language

- How to never run out of things to say

- Bonus chapters on Persuasion, Emotional Intelligence, and How to Analyze People

To grab your free bonus book just <u>tap here</u>, or go to:

<u>http://ryanjames.successpublishing.club/freebonus/</u>

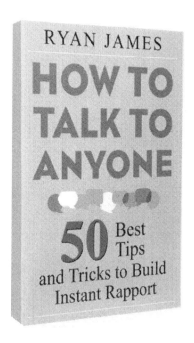

# CHAPTER 1

---

# COGNITIVE BEHAVIORAL
# THERAPY OVERVIEW

Has your life been robbed of beauty and fullness by fear? Are you tired of people telling you that the only way you can overcome your fears is to face them? While it is true that facing your fears is an effective way to overcome your fears, it is not the only way. In fact, there are other ways you can try to overcome your phobias, depression, and anxiety. One of these ways is rewiring your brain.

You see, your brain generally takes the easiest approach to deal with problems and that is fleeing. Fleeing is actually a learned response that is much easier than overcoming challenges and facing confrontations. Nevertheless, it is still possible to rewire the brain so that it responds differently to similar situations. Yes, it may require pain and dedication, but it is all worth it.

Throughout the years, your brain may have adopted certain ways such as fear, anxiety, panic, and worry; but all of these can be unlearned. You can rewire your brain to act the way you want it to so that it can successfully serve its purpose in your life.

For some people, the answer is COGNITIVE BEHAVIORAL THERAPY.

## What is CBT?

Put in the simplest terms, CBT is a goal-oriented, short-term treatment that actually takes a more hands-on approach when it comes to dealing with the issues that people have. The primary goal here is to basically rewire the brain—that is, change a person's pattern of thinking, and in doing so, also changed the way they feel. It is used to treat a number of different issues; this treatment can help with relationship problems, sleeping difficulties, and even drug or alcohol abuse.

Alright, let's talk about rewiring the brain again. CBT is able to do this by focusing on thoughts, beliefs, attitudes, and images that are held by the individual's cognitive processes. Keep in mind that how these processes happen relates to how that individual behaves as well and how they cope with emotional problems.

## Short-Term vs. Long Term

So, one of the more significant advantages that CBT has over other forms of treatment would be the fact that it is shorter in terms of duration. It usually lasts around five to ten months for most emotional issues that need to be treated.

A client would need to diligently attend one session every week, with each one lasting for about 50 minutes at a time. For the average individual, this is only a minimal chunk of time that they need to devote to it, but the results are worth every minute.

*What happens during a session?*

For the 50 minutes they spend in session, the client and therapist would work together in order to better understand what the real problems are. Once these have been properly identified, a new strategy for dealing with them is created—it is during this time that clients are usually introduced to a set of principles or philosophies which they can apply whenever needed. These are principles that is useful for any given situation and would last them a lifetime.

Cognitive Behavioral Therapy is a combination of **behavioral therapy** and **psychotherapy**. It takes psychotherapy's emphasis on the importance of the meaning we give certain things and the thinking patterns we form in childhood. From behavioral therapy, it derives the need to pay a closer attention to the relationship between the issues we have, our thoughts, and our overall behavior.

It must be noted that most psychotherapists who practice CBT will customize the treatment to the specific need of each individual client. Needless to say, there is no "one-size-fits-all" solution for everyone.

## CBT Benefits:

People who have specific problems tend to be the most suitable for CBT as its techniques tend to focus on very specific goals. Most experts agree that it isn't as suitable for people who feel vaguely unfulfilled or have fleeting moments of unhappiness. The same goes for people who do not have specific areas of their lives they want to work on and improve.

It is also more likely to benefit people who related to the ideas behind CBT as many of them can be very different from other types of treatment. It is a very problem-solving approach, and is meant for people who want a more practical treatment as opposed to gaining further insight into the self.

It is most effective for:

- Anxiety and panic attacks

- Anger Management

- Chronic Fatigue Syndrome

- Chronic Pain

- Drug and Alcohol Addiction

- Depression

- Mood Swings

- Eating Problems

- General Health Problems

- Bad Habits and Facial Tics

- Phobias

- PTSD

- OCD

- Sleep Problems

- Sexual and Relationship Problems

## Thoughts, Feelings and the Internal Dialogue

It was psychiatrist Aaron Beck who first realized the connection between an individual's thoughts and feelings, and that these two can significantly affect how a person behaves. The idea here is simple, imagine this scenario:

During a meeting with their bosses, an employee might think to themselves "My boss hasn't said much about my presentation. Are they displeased with it?" These thoughts can lead to the employee feeling anxious or distressed. In turn, they might continue thinking that, "Maybe they're simply distracted or perhaps, I haven't been providing enough interesting information to keep them focused." With that second thought, the employee's overall feelings might change.

These thoughts are what Beck refers to as "automatic thoughts", basically the ones that easily pop up in the mind when we're in situations that aren't comfortable. His studies show that most people are not aware of these thoughts, but they can learn how to identify and talk about them. Think about it for yourself; how many times have you found yourself upset and began thinking negative thoughts that were neither helpful nor realistic?

Negative thinking is automatic in these situations. Don't worry, it's totally normal. In fact, these could even be the key that would help you overcome your difficulties.

Cognitive Behavioral Therapy is meant to help you understand what is happening in your mind. It would enable you to view your automatic thoughts from a different perspective, basically giving you more insight into them. The thing is, negative and uncomfortable situations aren't things we can simply walk away from—but knowing how to deal with them properly is a good start.

Think of it as your first step towards breaking the pattern of you listening to your negative thoughts, and subsequently feeling discouraged because of it. Once you understand how it works, you would be able to separate yourself from these thoughts and figure out a solution to the dilemma you're currently facing. No, it won't be an easy road, but it certainly is doable.

So, where does one begin?

## CHAPTER 2

---

# BE AWARE OF COGNITIVE DISTORTIONS

These are your inaccurate thoughts that reinforce negative emotions and thoughts. Some people are quite prone to this, allowing the thoughts to convince them of a reality that is simply not true. For example:

"My officemate isn't replying to me. Maybe they're busy? Or is it because they don't like me and would rather not be bothered by my presence?"

If you aren't aware of cognitive distortions, you might easily believe the latter. However, it simply isn't true.

Here are some common distortions you must avoid:

## 1. Filtering.

This refers to a person's inability to see the good things that are also happening around them. Basically, they only dwell on the negative aspect of things, whether it be their own skill or the issue they're currently facing, and as such, they fail to see the other possibilities that may come from it. Many people are prone to this.

How do you overcome it? **Try making use of positive affirmations.**

Positive affirmations refer to the words that you tell yourself over and over until they become ingrained into your subconscious mind. They are practically messages that give you encouragement and motivation. They are also anti-negative self-talk. Hence, they can significantly improve your self-confidence and self-esteem.

The positive effects of positive affirmations are evident in a study featured in the Journal of American College Health. According to this study, female participants who applied cognitive behavioral techniques into their life, such as positive affirmations, were able to reduce negative thinking as well as alleviate symptoms of depression.

**How to Create Positive Affirmations**

The following are pointers that can help you create the most effective positive affirmations that will change your life:

1. Be mindful of the words, phrases, and sentences that you use. After all, you do not want to send out the wrong message to the universe and to yourself. Before you finalize your affirmations, see to it that you check the wordings and phrasings.

2. Keep in mind that your emotions are connected with your words. So, when you recite positive affirmations, your emotions follow suit. This is why you have to refrain from using words that can relate to negative emotions, such as 'hate'. You can replace these negative words with positive ones, such as 'love'.

3. Use the present tense. The subconscious mind is not able to differentiate positive and nega-

tive sentences because all it knows is the present. This is why you have to write and recite your positive affirmations in the present tense to get your desired effects.

4. Keep your mind calm, peaceful, and relaxed. If you want your positive affirmations to work, you have to recite them when your mind is clear so that it can easily absorb what you say. You must refrain from reciting affirmations if your mind is chaotic because this will send out the wrong messages to the universe and to yourself.

**Remember to Look at the Bigger Picture**

Experts say that in order for you to stay happy, you have to look at the big picture and not focus on the negatives. If you focus on the negatives, you will miss out on the positive aspects of things and you will not enjoy your life.

According to Paul Dubois, a Swiss psychiatrist, you have to get a piece of paper and draw a couple of columns on it. Then, you have to write down the things that trouble you as well as the things that make you happy. For everything that troubles you, you have to give it a happy counterpart. You have to do this exercise every night before you go to bed.

The main idea behind this exercise is to realize that you have positive things happening to you daily. For every bad experience you have, you will find a good experience. This will prevent you from merely focusing on the negatives and aggravating your depression or anxiety.

For example, if you arrive late for work, you may beat yourself up. You may think to yourself that you are going to get reprimanded by your boss and that you may have a bad record. However, something good can still come out of this. If you are religious, you can view it as God's way of sparing you from an accident or from an unpleasant situation.

If your fiancé left you at the altar, you may think that it is the end of the world; but it is not. You can either be depressed about this or view it as a blessing in disguise. You may have actually dodged a bullet by not marrying this person because you are meant to meet someone much better.

In doing this, you are training your mind to focus more on the positive and possibilities that may arise from difficulties. So each time you feel as if you're obsessing over the bad, make sure you do these exercises to remind yourself of the good as well.

## 2. Overgeneralization.

This is taking a single bad experience and using it as basis for how the others might turn out. Imagine this scenario: An individual is looking to get their art recognized. They have confidence in what they can do, but after a bad review, they began feeling discouraged and believe every negative criticism they were given. In the end, they refused to continue painting. Quite a waste, right? Don't let yourself fall into the same trap.

How do you overcome it? *Use the power of positive visualization.*

Visualization, which is also referred to as guided imagery, is another effective way to overcome any negative train of thought you might be having. In fact, it is also known to help people when it comes to dealing with their anxiety and depression—even phobias.

**The idea here is rather simple**. Every time you perform guided imagery or visualization, you imagine yourself in a place or time that relaxes you. If you are sick, you may also imagine yourself in a healthier state.

How does it work? Well, it replaces negative images in your mind with positive ones. Imagine the painter once more—this time, they're making use of visualization to help lessen the anxiety they feel over having to present their artworks. Through independent or guided visualization, they evoke images of an applauding crowd, even the biggest critics they have are wearing a smile and nodding their approval.

Their pieces are hung in some of the biggest galleries and in time, they get offers from people who wish to purchase them. All of that could be achieved if they simply took that important step of picking up their paintbrush again and looking past the negative review they were given.

It's such a simple practice, but it can be powerful enough to help restore an individual's confidence and replace the negative images they might have previously had in their minds.

Guided imagery or visualization is actually a form of meditative practice. It involves the use of words, visualizations, and/or music that encourages positive images to appear in the mind and create the desired effects on the body. It can energize or calm your body, as well as help eliminate your negative thoughts and emotions.

## 3. Personalization.

This is a kind of cognitive distortion that has individuals believing that everything they do actually impacts people and other external events. It doesn't matter how irrational the link may seem, the belief is stronger than logic. The person who suffers from this distortion would always feel as if they had a role in the bad events that happen around them.

For example, they may feel as if the company meeting was unsuccessful because they were late to it—despite the fact that their role in said meeting is particularly minor compared to other people's. This is also what happens in children who tend to blame themselves for the separation of their parents. They begin to believe that it is somewhat their fault and that, perhaps, if they were a better child, then it wouldn't have happened.

How do you overcome it? **Remind yourself that not everything is under your control**, and that sometimes, unless you were directly involved then the blame is not on you. Now, this would be difficult if the individual has gotten used to this pattern of thinking, but with practice it is certainly something that can be easily dealt with.

Take for example a friend of mine who experiences this ever so often. In order to avoid obsessing over the situation, what they do is take a 5 minute break to mentally list down possible solutions to the problem at hand. In doing this exercise, they are able to distract themselves and the feeling eventually passes. The productivity is a plus, and in some cases, they were able to come up with great suggestions for their entire team as well.

Remember, not everything is under your control, and despite your mistakes, you are not always to blame for things not going as they're supposed to.

## 4. Emotional Reasoning.

This distortion often leads people into thinking that if they feel it, then it must be true. For example, if you feel uninteresting or unappealing in a given moment, then it must be why people are not giving you any attention.

But does this line of thinking actually apply? Of course not. Our emotions will not always be an accurate indication of the truth. However, these feelings might be difficult to overlook for some. This is especially true if there are already underlying thoughts that further feed this emotion, insecurities that they may not have voiced out before, but have constantly been in their minds.

Again, we go back to: OUR THOUGHTS AFFECT OUR FEELINGS.

How do we overcome it? ***Challenge your emotional reasoning***:

It will be a bit difficult at first, but it is the first step. Look at your situation and analyze how you're reacting to it. Perhaps the reason why no one's talking to you is because you're not putting in enough effort to connect with people. Say you're with a group, you'll easily feel left out if you don't participate in the ongoing conversation. Speak your thoughts every now and then or agree with an opinion that matches yours.

You cannot expect people to do all the work for you. If you remain hidden at a party, then the chances of you meeting new friends is very slim. The same goes if you maintain a stance that's a bit off putting—body posture speaks too. Try and be more open, you need not make a big splash or put on a show. Do what you're comfortable with when it comes to changing the situation; challenge your reasoning by testing your thoughts out.

## 5. Fallacy of Fairness.

More often than not, we are concerned with fairness and everyone getting the equal share. However, in this case, it is taken to the extremes. It is a fact of life that things do not always go our way—it will not always be fair. People who have this distortion tend to look for fairness in every experience they have, often ending up unhappy and resentful of the world, as well as the people around them.

For example, people tend to think that kindness will be rewarded with kindness. Say, you allowed someone to get ahead of you in a queue thinking that this would be reciprocated the next time you're in a rush. However, you are only met with rejection and judgment when you do give it a try.

Life is unfair! This will be your first thought—no, it would be most people's. It might leave you distressed and angry. Some people even become disillusioned the more it occurs, thinking that everyone is against them and that the world is simply unkind. Sounds dramatic? Not at all. There are people who think this way, and it is also one of the reasons why some of them end up becoming depressed.

How do you overcome it? Whilst you cannot change the world overnight, there are some changes that you can apply to yourself. The first of which would be reminding yourself that life will not always go your way EVEN if you put an effort into always doing things right. Do not expect to be rewarded for your deeds, and instead, simply do them because, well, the world needs more of it.

Each time you find yourself in an unfair situation, look at it and try to find the possibilities. There's always something positive in any negative situation, you just have practice changing how you look at them.

## 6. Fallacy of Change.

This refers to an individual's irrational expectation that other people would change according to what suits them. Basically, this means that our overall happiness becomes dependent on how other people act, and in their unwillingness to "cooperate" despite being pushed to or demanded to hinder us from feeling fulfilled. This is a truly damaging way to think and can cause depression and relationship issues, especially since no one else is responsible for our own happiness other than ourselves.

Ask yourself: Are the people around you providing you with positive encouragement? Are they focused on developing as individuals or are they simply hanging on to you because they gain some form of benefit?

The truth of the matter is this: There are cases wherein we find ourselves with a group of people purely out of convenience—because they're there. They do not contribute to our development as people nor do we influence them positively. In such scenarios, both parties might develop certain expectations that remain unfulfilled simply because their personalities, development as individuals, and overall path no longer match up.

It may also be that you're surrounding yourself with people who demand so much of you or whose expectations you keep trying to live up to, but feel as if you're unable to do so. This can cause feelings of inadequacy to take root and with that, lowered self-confidence, anxiety, and depression.

There's nothing wrong about outgrowing the company you keep. It happens to everyone and in some cases, it is much healthier to cut ties instead of hanging on to them. REMEMBER: You are responsible for your own happiness and as such, if you must take action, then YOU need to start now.

**PRO TIP: Surround Yourself with Optimistic People**

If you want to be free from depression and anxiety, you have to keep your circle happy. Negative people are toxic to your wellbeing because their negativity can wear off on you. Keep in mind that both positivity and negativity are contagious. Whoever you surround yourself with can have a great impact on your mindset and attitude. This is why successful people surround themselves with other successful people. Likewise, those who want to succeed in life find people who may influence them in a positive sense.

The same thing applies if you want to overcome depression, anxiety, and phobias. You have to choose your company wisely. If all you see all day are people who are sad, depressed, and blaming the world for their problems, you too will be like them pretty soon. Nevertheless, even though you cannot control the way they think and behave, you can still control the way you treat them. You can also control the way you react towards their negativity.

It would be nice to try to help these people change for the better. You can try to influence and encourage them to change their ways and be more positive. However, you just cannot force anyone to do something that they do not want to do. They have to be willing to help themselves. A lot of negative people are not even aware that they are toxic to others. So, if you want to save yourself and maintain your sanity, the best thing to do is simply walk away and stay away from them as much as possible.

People can only be helped if they really want to be helped. If they try to drag you into their drama, you must walk away. Rather than answer or fight back, you should just focus on your own thing. You must focus on yourself, your goals, and the things that can help you grow better as a person. You have to let go of the negative people in your life if you want to be happy and stress free.

You have to take care of yourself, which means that you have to take good care of your physical and mental health. Remember that your mind affects your body. So, if you do not have a healthy mind, you will have an unhealthy body as well. This is why you have to surround yourself with people who are beneficial to your mental wellness. You should only hang out with people who inspire, encourage, and support you.

Negative people are toxic to your sanity. If you have friends who are negative, you should cut them from your life, even if you have known them for a long time. If you have co-workers who do nothing but gossip and pick on other people, you should stay as far away from them as you can. Do not talk to them unless you really have to and it is solely about work. These people will only drag you down to their level and you do not want that.

## 7. Catastrophizing.

This refers to the individual who is always expecting the worst possible thing that could happen even if the situation is minor or nowhere near the level of tragedy they're picturing. For example, you have a fear of water and despite the countless safety measures put in place, you still believe that something will go wrong. In your head, that waist-deep water can still drown you.

**How to overcome it?** Face up to your fears and expose yourself to them.

In doing so, you'll be able to see the reality of the situation instead of creating negative scenarios in your head. An effective way to get over your fears is to gradually face them until you become more aware of the fact that IT'S ALL IN YOUR HEAD. The more exposure you get the more familiar you become with the fear. This lessens its impact on you. So for example, if you want to be more comfortable with public speaking or negotiating, you can undergo exposure therapy.

Katherina Hauner, a neuroscientist from the Rehab Institute of Chicago, said that exposure therapy dramatically improves the way patients view their fears. This treatment method is typically performed in hierarchical steps. The series starts with a low level of engagement and increases with every step. For example, if you have a fear of water, try starting with shallow pools and gradually make your way to the deeper end.

**The Right Amount of Exposure**

In order for exposure therapy to work for you, you have to have just the right amount of exposure. You have to enter the situation with a clear goal to avoid making your anxiety worse.

Keep in mind that exposing yourself to a situation does not automatically mean having to walk into a room and standing idly. You have to ask yourself how you have to behave in this kind of situation. When you expose yourself to new situations and yet you still behave the way you did in the past, you will only end up feeling anxious again because you are just reconditioning yourself to do so.

This is why you have to act differently when you expose yourself to a different situation. If you are faced with a new situation and yet your actions are still the same, you expose yourself to the situation and avoid it at the same time. This prevents you from fully exposing yourself and allowing you to overcome anxiety.

Let's go back to our example. Instead of saying to getting in the water, try doing it bit by bit. If you feel more comfortable if you wear a life-vest then do so! The important thing here is to actually make the first step and changing your usual pattern of saying NO. This time, say YES to the experience. Sure, you may not overcome your fear after one try, but there is power in conquering that first level.

## How to Expose Yourself to Challenges and Situations

Keep in mind that exposure requires proper planning and timing. You need to condition yourself and make a commitment to overcoming your depression, anxiety, and phobias.

You need to create a list of all the things that make you fearful, just as the one you have read previously in this book. You have to include everything, whether they are objects, situations, places, or people. You have to be as clear and specific as possible, writing down every detail that involves your fear.

Consider your environment. Some people feel more anxious about swimming in a lake while others feel more anxious about swimming in a pool. When you swim in a lake, you have less control of your environment. On the other hand, when you swim in a pool, there are lifeguards and you are also more aware of the water's depth.

**The Fear Ladder**

Then, you have to face your fears. You have also read about this earlier. You can start facing the fears that are at the bottom of your Fear Ladder or the ones that give you the least amount of anxiety. At first, you may spend only a few seconds or minutes facing your fears. As you become less anxious about it, you may spend more time facing such fears until you no longer fear them.

Every time you perform exposure exercise, you can track your level of fear. You can stay in the fearful situation until your fear level goes down by fifty percent. For example, if carrying a knife has a rating of 6/10 on your Fear Scale, you can continue carrying it until your level of fear drops down to just 3/10.

You also have to plan performing exposure exercises ahead of schedule so that you can have more control over your situations as well as easily determine what you have to do. Do not forget to keep track of your progress. Compare your situations before and after to see how far you have come as well as find out about the things you have learned along the way.

Regular practice is also necessary.

You also have to maintain your gains even if you have already gotten comfortable about doing something. You should not stop exposing yourself to your feared situation so that your fears do not return. For example, if you have successfully overcome your fear of the water, go swimming regularly. Do not let a long time pass by before you give it a try again as this might be detrimental to your progress.

Remember, the more familiar you make yourself with your fears the less you'll catastrophize the situation.

# CHAPTER 3

# EMPLOY CBT TOOLS AND MAXIMIZE THEM

There are many simple tools that can help you understand your thoughts better, as well as what they might be rooted at. It is important that you use and maximize them in order to fully immerse yourself in the treatment. In this chapter, we present you with some of the most common CBT tools and how you can use them better.

## 8. Journaling.

Think of journaling as a means of gathering data about your thoughts and your different moods. When writing in your journal, always try to expand on the mood or thought. Answer some of these questions:

1.  *What was the source?*

2.  *How intense was the thought or the mood?*

3.  *How did you respond to it?*

This tool can help you better identify your emotional tendencies and thought patterns. Having a record enables you to look back as well, and look at everything from an outsider's perspective. A journal helps prevent you from being in your head too much as well—this can lead to negative thinking if you're not careful.

### The Benefits of Starting a Journal

Journaling is a relaxing and effective way to express thoughts and emotions freely, without worrying about hurting others or being scrutinized. After all, you are the only one who gets to read your thoughts when you put it on paper. You can say everything you want without inhibitions on your journal. Hence, you can get things off your chest without making a fool of yourself in public.

You can keep your journal hidden to keep your entries secret or start an online journal that is available to the public. Do not worry because even if your virtual journal is available for all Internet users to see, you still get to keep your anonymity, just as long as you do not publish personal information such as your full name, address, and contact details. You may also want to change the names of the people involved so as to protect their identities.

Then again, this may be too much work for you, especially if you do not have time to edit names or use code names. An advantage of using a virtual journal is that you get to have unlimited space. You can write as many entries as you want, and you do not have to buy a new journal. In addition, you do not have to worry about misplacing your journal and having someone else find and read it. You can also write from anywhere, as long as you bring your computer with you.

Journaling lets you communicate with the areas of your psyche that have been frozen; thus, allowing you to tap into the deeper reserves of problem solving and creativity. When you write in a journal, you are able to gain a flash of awareness and knowing that you have not yet seen before. This enables you to gain clarity and reduce any feelings of depression or anxiety.

According to Dr. Michael Rank, co-director and associate professor at the International Traumatology Institute of the University of South Florida, journaling forces you to act and do something. Dr. Jessie Gruman, executive director at the Center for the Advancement of Health in Washington, agrees that journaling is an excellent way to cope with depression and anxiety.

What's more, journaling gives you a chance to see your feelings in black and white. More often than not, you judge your feeling and thoughts subjectively. This is not healthy because you may have the wrong interpretation. When you write down your thoughts, you can pause or reread them, allowing you to reflect and properly figure out how to deal with them.

## 9. Make Room for Pleasant Activity Scheduling.

The idea here is to indulge yourself in an activity that stimulates positive feelings in you. For some, this could be a good book and a good cup of coffee, for others it could be catching up with friends. What's important is that it must be an activity that's healthy for you—so, no binge eating or smoking. These things might stimulate the pleasure sensors in your brain, but they can actually worsen your overall state of mind.

Sugar can cause energy crashes. Smoking can cause addictions.

A good option to try here is creating a regular exercise routine for yourself. Regular, as in, something you do quite often if you cannot manage to do it everyday.

### The Benefits of Exercising:

The physical and mental benefits of exercise have long been established. All experts agree that regular exercise can help fight against diseases and improve overall wellness. Exercise is not only good for your physical body, but for your mental health as well.

Numerous studies have shown that exercise can reduce fatigue, enhance overall cognitive function, improve concentration, and increase alertness. With this being said, regular exercise can help you focus better as well as increase your energy levels. More importantly, it can help you manage your stress and anxiety levels.

When stress affects the brain, along with its nerve connections, the body feels the same negative impact. This is why you need to condition both your mind and body when you are stressed or anxious. Since your body gets pumped up with adrenaline during moments of stress and anxiety, you need to put this adrenaline rush towards physical activity, such as aerobic exercises, to make you feel better.

Furthermore, scientists say that regular aerobic exercises can significantly reduce levels of tension, improve sleep, boost self-esteem, and increase and stabilize mood levels. So, even if you are too busy with work and you do not have time to go to the gym, you can still exercise. You can perform exercises in five minutes and still reap the same good benefits as you would when you spend half an hour to one hour at the gym.

### *What Exercise Does:*

It is no secret that exercise is indeed effective in keeping yourself fit, healthy, and happy. The following are the immediate effects of exercise to your mind and body:

- It pumps up endorphins. When you engage in any physical activity, you encourage the production of endorphins. This enables your mood to quickly shift from angry, sad, or frustrated to happy, calm, and optimistic.

- It gives you the benefits of meditation, something that is also important when it comes to CBT as **it keeps you from ruminating**. Exercise can be regarded as meditation in motion. It requires mental focus just like meditation, but with the added body movement. When you exercise, you have to focus on your breathing, movement, and posture leaving no room for negative thinking.

- It serves as a positive distraction. If you are stressed or anxious, you can engage in active sports such as racquetball and swimming, or play any other fast-paced game. Afterwards, you will realize that you no longer feel as irritated and grumpy as before. This happens because exercise also serves as a positive distraction. So rather than stay consumed by worries, you become forced to focus on movement.

- It improves your mood. When you exercise on a regular basis, you improve your self-confidence levels. Physical activity can help achieve relaxation as well as reduce the symptoms related to anxiety and depression. Exercise can also help you sleep better at night so that you can rest and wake up feeling refreshed and rejuvenated.

If you want something a little less physically tasking or if something is preventing you from exercising, you can also opt for mindfulness meditation. It can provide you with the same mental benefits as exercising and can leave you feeling better, and much clearer.

## 10. Mindfulness Meditation.

There's a wide range of benefits to this, but it is one of the most effective CBT techniques when it comes to dealing with <u>AUTOMATIC THOUGHTS</u>. It enables you to disengage from obsessing and rumination, allowing you to stay grounded. In this manner, your feelings and behavior would not be swayed by any of the negativity that may go on in your mind.

### The Benefits of Mindfulness Meditation

Numerous studies have shown that mindfulness meditation is effective in managing depression, pain, and anxiety. It is about training the brain to focus on the present moment instead of the regrets from the past or anxieties towards the future.

Whenever you worry, you focus more on what might happen in the future and what you have to do about it. This can make you anxious and stressed. Through mindfulness meditation, you can break free from these worries and bring your attention back to your present.

Mindfulness is about observing your thoughts and acknowledging them before finally letting them go. It refers to your ability to stay aware of your current feelings as well as moment-to-moment external and internal experiences.

When you practice mindfulness meditation, you are able to determine where your thinking causes problems. It also helps you get in touch better with your emotions. In essence, mindfulness is about acknowledging and observing your anxious feelings and thoughts, letting go of your worries, and staying focused on the present moment.

Mindfulness meditation can help you stay focused and calm in the present so that you are able to bring balance back to your nervous system. Mindfulness meditation has long been practiced in different parts of the world to reduce anxiety, stress, and depression among other mental health issues.

## Getting Started

Before you can practice mindfulness meditation, you need to find a quiet environment first. Ideally, you must choose a place that is secluded, quiet, and peaceful. This can be anywhere – in your home, in the woods, or at a temple. Whatever place you choose, it has to be relaxing and free from any interruptions or distractions.

You also have to allot a specific time for your meditation practice. According to experts, the most ideal hours are early in the morning, particularly between 3 o'clock and five o'clock in the morning. The ancient teachers and practitioners of meditation said that it is during these hours that the mind is at its most re-freshed state. They add that the mind is like a blank slate which you can easily fill with positive and help-ful thoughts.

In addition, meditating in the morning helps you prepare for the long day ahead. In the evening, med-itating allows you to clear your mind and get rid of the stressful things that happened throughout the day. It also prepares you for a good night's sleep so that you can wake up feeling refreshed and rejuve-nated the next day.

Having specific schedules for practicing mindfulness meditation helps you form consistent habit. The more often you do it, the more automatic it becomes. You can set your timer or alarm clock at a specific hour. Pretty soon, you will no longer think or plan about practicing mindfulness meditation because your body will automatically go to your meditation room and you will start meditating.

You will feel the need to meditate upon waking up in the morning and before going to bed at night. Habits are hard to break, which is why you need to make meditating a solid habit.

1. Begin by finding a comfortable position. When you meditate, you should feel comfortable when you sit. If you are not comfortable, you will not be able to focus on meditating. Make sure that you wear comfortable clothes as well. Choose clothes that are loose, light, and breathable so you can move freely.

2. You can sit on the floor or in a chair, whichever feels more comfortable for you. There are different sitting positions you can choose from. For example, you can choose full lotus, half lotus, or quarter lotus.

3. If you are using an alarm clock to help you keep track of the time, you should place it near you but not too near that it might distract you. You also have to position its face away from you so that you will not be tempted to check the time every now and then. This can be distracting from your meditation session.

4. Do not forget your point of focus. This can be anything, whether real or imaginary. If you prefer to meditate with your eyes open, you can stare at an object as your point of focus.

For example, you can stare at the flame of a candle or at a point on the wall.

5.  If you prefer to meditate with your eyes closed, you can visualize your point of focus. For example, you can imagine seeing a ray of light. You can also select a mantra or a phrase or word with a special meaning. If you have a mantra, you have to repeat it throughout your meditation session.

It is important that you have a non-critical and observant attitude towards mindfulness meditation. You should not worry about harboring distracting thoughts because it is normal for beginners to have wandering minds. If distracting thoughts come across your mind, you should just let them be. You should not try to fight them, but rather gently bring your attention back to your point of focus.

## 11.  Cognitive Reframing.

Cognitive reframing or restructuring is one of the core parts of CBT. It is also considered to be a very effective treatment when it comes to common issues that people face, including: anxiety disorders, binge eating, and depression.

How to do it? It's basically taking something that's making you feel bad, and turning it into something that's good. Let's take anxiety for example.

## Reframing Anxiety as Excitement

When you reframe your anxiety as excitement, you are able to devote more resources and energy to the situation. According to Alison Wood, an assistant professor at Harvard Business School, the most ideal way to deal with anxiety is to get excited. This finding is in contrast to the belief of most people, which is to keep calm.

You see, your emotions occur at two levels: arousal and valence. Arousal refers to the physical sensation that occurs in the psych world while valence refers to the way you interpret this arousal mentally.

Whenever you become anxious, your heart rate soars. When this happens, you experience high arousal, and that is a negative valence. So, whenever you feel anxious, you have to reframe it as a feeling of excitement instead of dwelling upon it with feelings of dread. By reframing it, your heart rate soars, but with it comes positive feelings instead of restlessness.

Moreover, researchers have found that those who re-frame their anxiety as excitement are able to become better when it comes to dealing with the subject of their problem. These people tend to have higher confidence levels, which are beneficial for success. They also tend to be more optimistic and friendly, traits that can get you far in life. So, the next time you feel anxious, you should find something to be excited about.

### Recognize that You Are Doing Alright

Everyday, you have to recognize that you are doing alright. During random moments of your day, you have to take a pause and congratulate yourself for being fine.

Rick Hanson, a neuropsychologist who writes for Psychology Today, says that your instincts for survival make you constantly fearful and unsettled. While these instincts protect you by preventing you from letting your guard down completely, they also make you anxious.

Feeling anxious? Tell yourself that everything is alright, and that it is okay to be feeling this way. It's only natural—after all, you're doing something huge and

EXCITING. Do not let the feeling dictate negativity into your mind. Use it instead as a fuel by reminding yourself that you're doing just fine.

## 12. Write Down Self-Affirmations.

This may seem similar to reciting positive affirmations, but there is one distinct difference and that is THE TOPIC OF YOUR AFFIRMATIONS. This exercise centers on you as an individual and on your core values—ones you may have formed during your childhood. These are the ones that have the strongest association to feelings of positivity, especially if they are somehow related to your family.

For example: If you're find yourself having a bout with anxiety before presenting an new idea to the company, tell yourself "My mother always taught me that there are no big challenges, only people who are not up to the task." Repeat that thought until the negative thought is gone and you're only filled with these encouraging words.

Always make sure that you affirm core values before any challenging situations, especially if you start feeling terrified or plagued by thoughts of failure, and rejection. By doing this, you can stay positive in any situation.

So, the next time you go to a job interview or face a difficult situation, you have to pause for a while and remember your core values. Take a deep breath and recall the values that you grew up with.

These core values may be about your family, relationships, creativity, or career success among others. You have to select one of these values and determine why it is important for you. Get a piece of paper and write down your reasons as to why they are important. You have to be as vivid as possible.

Psychologists and researchers both agree that it can help reduce stress and anxiety. In a study that involved eighty-five undergraduate students, it was found that writing about core values helps reduce stress levels.

The participants were told to give five-minute speeches as members of the audience yelled at them to speak faster. Before they gave their speeches, however, the participants selected the value that they thought to be most important as well as the value that they thought to be quite irrelevant. Then, they half-wrote about such values.

Sure enough, those who have written about their highest rated values were found to be less stressed out during their speech. They also had lower levels of cortisol than those who wrote about their lowest rated values.

## 13.   Imagery Based Exposure.

This exercise would involve you recalling a recent memory that produced an intense feeling of negativity within you. Now, once you have it in mind, analyze the situation.

For example, you found yourself in a distressing situation at work where you ended up arguing with one of your officemates. They might have said something hurtful that left you reeling and completely out of it.

Yes, the exercise might bring back some of those feelings, but try focusing on the purpose at hand instead of those emotions. Remind yourself that the situation has passed and now, you're merely studying it to gain a better understanding of how you reacted.

Next, label the thoughts and emotions that you went through during the conflict. Identify and write them down.

How does this help? Well, by visualizing this situation, it can actually help you take away its power to trigger the same emotions in you. Exposing yourself again to those negative feelings and urges will take some of its ability to affect you once more.

## 14.    Thought Recording.

For this exercise, you will be testing out the validity of your thoughts. Basically, this would involve having to gather and then analyzing any evidence for and against a thought you might have. What this enables you to see is a fact-based conclusion on whether said thought is valid or not.

For example, you might think that your boss thinks low of you and that they find you inadequate for the job. You would need to gather all the evidence that makes you believe this is true, such as "They weren't smiling as I was making my presentation and he asked many questions as if to embarrass me." Then think of evidence that is against this belief, such as

"They did give me a pat on the back after the presentation" and "They also told me to keep it up. If they thought ill of me, then they wouldn't have encouraged me in that way."

The goal here is to create a more balanced picture in your mind, as well as get rid of the unreasonable negative thoughts that you have formed prior.

For example, "Perhaps my boss was listening intently to my presentation hence why they did not smile much and asked many questions. I should listen instead to their encouragement, and keep up what I'm doing to become a better employee."

# CHAPTER 4

# THE IMPORTANCE OF SELF-TALK

We all have an inner critic and it tends to be louder and more persistent whenever we find ourselves feeling anxious or depressed. This is the voice in our head that constantly berates us and feeds us with negative statements—unfortunately, some of us tend to listen to it more than the positive voice. It is true, we are our own worse critics and the way we talk to ourselves can significant affect how we feel and how we deal with certain situations.

Have you ever heard it say things like:

- "I am so useless."

- "I am not good enough for this."

- "I am so dull and boring. This is why people find me invisible."

- "I am not pretty enough."

- "I will never find happiness."

- "I am too much for other people. This is why they leave me."

Sound familiar? Well, you're not alone. As awful as this voice is, there is a way of "silencing" it. What you must first understand is that our self-image and self-esteem is actually developed by the way we speak to ourselves. Whilst this inner self-critic believes it's protecting us from disappointments, it actually is making things worse.

Have you ever heard of the "ego defense mechanism"? This would be part of it. However, none of its criticisms is constructive—instead, it attacks us and stops many people from living their lives to the fullest. This is why it's important to study the way we talk to ourselves and fix the faults in it.

Self-talk refers to the way you talk to yourself. In general, people talk to themselves at a rate of 150 to 300 words per minute or roughly 50,000 times a day.

Your self-talk of internal thinking occurs through your mind's conscious area, and you may not be aware that your self-talk becomes instructions to your subconscious mind. The main task of your subconscious mind is to fulfill the orders sent to it by your conscious mind. Your subconscious mind is also your own personal servo-mechanism that works on your behalf non-stop.

### How Self Talk Works

If you want to understand better how self-talk works, you can think of an ocean liner. Imagine this ocean liner crossing the sea. The ship's captain barks orders to his crew, but the crew is in the hold of the ship. They are situated below the waterline, preventing them from seeing the direction of the ship.

You can consider the captain of the ship as your conscious mind and the crew as your subconscious mind. When the captain yells at the crew to go full speed ahead, the crew obeys just as they were told. They carry out the orders and have faith in their captain even though they cannot really see where they are heading. They do not think of the possibility of the ship colliding with another ship or with rocks. They do not question the judgment of their captain; they merely obey.

This is basically how your conscious and subconscious minds work. These two are not really separate. Instead, they are more of individual spheres of a singular mind. Whatever you tell yourself consciously has a direct effect on your subconscious mind.

If you engage in negative self-talk, your subconscious mind will receive the negative message and carry it out. On the other hand, if you engage in positive self-talk, you will have positive results.

Just like the crew of the ship in the above given example, your subconscious mind does not question the orders of your conscious mind. Whatever the conscious mind says, the subconscious mind receives without judgment.

### The Science of Self Talk

David Sarwer, clinical director and psychologist at the Center for Wright and Eating Disorders at the

University of Pennsylvania, uses a large mirror when dealing with his patients. He makes them stand in front of this mirror and tells them to use neutral and gentle language when evaluating their bodies.

For example, a patient who is overweight should opt to say that his abdomen is big, round, and bigger than he likes it to be, rather than his abdomen is grotesque and disgusting. According to Sarwer, his goal is to get rid of the pejorative and negative terms in the self-talk of his patients. He adds that it is not enough for his patients to lose or gain weight along. They also have to change the way they view their bodies so that they can maintain their ideal weight once they reach it.

In 2013, scientists from the Netherlands did a study that involved women with anorexia as participants. They observed these anorexic women walk through the doorways of the laboratory. They noticed that the women turned sideways and squeezed themselves into the doorways even though there is a lot of space available around them. These anorexic women apparently had a notion that their bodies are much bigger than they actually are.

In a similar study conducted in 1911, neurologists Dr. Gordon Morgan Holmes and Dr. Henry Head, published a series of studies discussing the connection of the brain and the body. They found that women who often wore huge hats with feathers on them ducked each time they walked through doorways. They did this even when they were not wearing the hats. In their mind, they were still wearing the hats.

According to Dr. Branch Coslett, a cognitive neuroscientist at the University of Pennsylvania, each person has an internal representation of their own body. You need this part of yourself so that you can understand and learn how much space you take up. This also helps you do and complete your tasks better and faster.

Researchers have also found that such internal sense is very powerful. Neurologists have done research on motor imagery, which shows that the same neurological networks are both used in imagining movement and actually moving. So, imagining a certain movement repeatedly can have a similar effect on your brain as actually doing it.

## Why Self Talk Matters

People do not always get what they want in life because they get what they expect and attract. Your self-talk actually creates your self-concept. It is your self-concept that identifies your level of performance in the different aspects of your life.

You can have over a hundred different individual self-concepts. For example, you may have a high self-concept of yourself during social events and situations. You may tell yourself that you are an excellent conversationalist and that you make good jokes. On the contrary, you may also have a low self-concept. You may tell yourself that you are not going to be promoted at work or that there are a lot of people who are smarter than you.

You should know that your subconscious works hard to make sure that your performance stays consistent with your self-concept, whether it is negative or positive. This is why you have to opt for the positive instead of the negative if you want your life to get better.

## 15.    Positive Self-Talk Counts.

Positive self-talk is regarded as the physical manifestation of the psyche, which provides encouragement. However, the researchers have found that the thoughts of an average person consist of 80% negativity and only 20% positivity. You should practice self-talk more often because they come with a lot of benefits.

-   **Positive self-talk can help reduce stress and anxiety levels.**

    Whenever you feel like you are being overwhelmed or stressed out, you can practice positive self-talk to uplift your spirits and make your mood better instantly. The American Heart Association says that stress control is one of the greatest benefits of positive self-talk.

-   **By reassuring yourself that things are going to be all right, you become less anxious and much calmer.**

    Then again, you have to take note that positive self-talk is not the same as lying to yourself about the real state of things. When you give yourself positive self-talk, you still have to be consistent with the reality. Things will only get worse if you lie to yourself and believe such lies.

*Imagine this scenario:*

If your husband just divorced you, you cannot lie to yourself that your relationship will magically return to the way it was. You should not fool yourself into thinking that you did not have problems. If you get back together, you will realize that things have gotten worse. This is why you still have to stay realistic. You can tell yourself that you will eventually get through the pain and move on with your life. This self-talk is positive yet realistic. It allows you to deal with your situation effectively and prevents you from making foolish decisions.

- **Positive self-talk also protects the heart and heart muscles.**

Stress, as you know, is among the most common causes of heart diseases. Since positive self-talk can reduce stress, it can also reduce your risk of heart diseases. This is proven by a study done by Susanne Pedersen, researcher at Tillburg University in Netherlands. According to the study, the participants who maintained a positive outlook in life had lower risks of mortality for the next five years.

- **Positive self-talk prevents depression and anxiety.**

Oftentimes, the people who are depressed feel worthless, hopeless, and useless. This affects both their minds and bodies, which is why they tend to experience eating problems, lethargy, and lack of sleep. If you give yourself a positive pep talk every now and then, you will stay happy and stress-free.

- **Positive self-talk can also increase your confidence.**

Lack of self-efficacy and negativity are two great hindrances to fulfilling your tasks. When you start to doubt your abilities, you set limits on the things that you are capable of doing. For example, if you are afraid of failing your exam or messing up your presentation, then you already set yourself up for failure. Negative self-talk attracts negative and undesirable results.

- **Positive self-talk can solidify and strengthen your belief in your own self.**

For example, if you truly believe that you can win the debate or get perfect scores on your exams, then you already prepared yourself for the outcome; which is winning the debate or acing your exams.

It is worth noting that your relationship with yourself is not the only thing that benefits when you give yourself a positive self-talk. You are also able to form better relationships with other people. This is because you become a reflection of positivity. Eventually, your positivity starts to spread to the people you are with. You start to recognize the good traits of your family, friends, peers, and co-workers, and ignore their less attractive traits. You become a more approachable person who is fun to be around.

Furthermore, positive self-talk can help improve your performance in different areas of life. For example, it is a vital part of sports psychology. When athletes practice positive self-talk, they are able to lessen their performance anxiety and pre-race jitters. Positive self-talk enables them to prepare for their event better as well as improve their overall performance. Likewise, positive self-talk can help you get ready for anything that you are about to face or undertake.

# CHAPTER 5

## SITUATIONAL CBT EXERCISES

### 16.    Behavioral Experiments.

These are done in order to test the validity of certain negative thoughts that you might be having, as well as any underlying beliefs to them. For example, in school, you often find yourself having a difficult time when it comes to saying no to your friends. We've all been here, haven't we? There is always some degree of peer pressure that happens in which we all think that saying NO might cause us our friends and people won't like us anymore.

One underlying fear here would be that of exclusion. We were afraid to say no because we did not want to end up an outsider. Besides, what could go wrong if we said YES? Plenty—this is what your adult self would say.

Behavioral experiments are a lot like the typical experiment you would do in class. Through it, you will be testing out a hypothesis. Will your friends really think ill of you should you say NO to them?

Test this on someone close to you. Tell them NO and then observe what happens next. Gather information and study how they react to it. Ask yourself these questions:

- Did they really end up liking you much less?

- How are you able to tell?

- Are you certain that this isn't just a false assumption?

After this, you can try doing the experiment again, but this time, do it with one of your friends. Say NO to them and see what happens and what's different this time.

In doing this, you're able to present yourself with evidence that disproves your negative thinking and subsequently tackles the underlying belief that's associated with it as well. There would be no fear of rejection after you realize that you were worried for nothing.

## 17.  Nightmare Exposure and Rescripting.

Here's the thing, anxieties and fears aren't always confined to when people are awake. Whilst sleep is comforting thought to some, there are people who dread having to close their eyes at night because of the nightmares that tend to accompany their slumber.

At its very core, this exercise is meant to help you face your fears and strip them of their ability to bring your grief. It is similar to other exposure exercises with some minor differences. This technique goes hand in hand with rescripting.

How to:

- Confront your nightmares. Remember that just like stories, these nightmares can have a number of different interpretations, too, and they are not always negative. Instead of avoiding sleep, remind yourself of this, and try to look at your nightmare from a new perspective. What do these monsters represent?

- It helps to write things down. Doing so may not be as easy since you have to recall things that have frightened you, but it would enable you to look at things clearly. Are there common themes between your nightmares?

- Analyze the details of your nightmare and focus on the experience.

- Once you've got all these things written, it's time to visualize a new story. This time, focus on the things you want to feel while dreaming. Change the frightening events into something better, let your imagination run wild. When it comes to dreams, you can do just about anything.

- TELL YOURSELF THAT YOU HAVE COMPLETE POWER OF THIS.

- It is important that you begin light. Never start with your worst nightmares. Instead work your way up, eventually you'll get to the point where even your worst nightmares no longer affect you and you can easily transform them into something else.

## 18.    Play the Script Until the End.

Think of this technique as a rehearsal for when the worst case scenario does happen. Sounds terrifying, it sort of is meant to be—after all, it is mimicking one of your worst fears. That said, the point of this technique is to help you avoid becoming crippled by your phobias and your anxieties. Through it, you'll be able to examine what could happen in the worst possible scenario you can conjure up.

Alright, where to begin? Again, start small. Save the worst fears for later and make sure you work your way up slowly, but steadily.

For example, one of my worst fears is driving off the road and somehow ending into a deep body of water. In this scenario, I am so crippled by fear that all I can do is watch as my vehicle slowly sinks. Of course, this isn't what I want to happen.

To put this technique to use, I imagine myself seating in that car and remembering all the things I have learned while researching. There is a way out and as long as I follow what I know, it'll be okay. I have a few minutes to get everything done, all I need to do is stay calm and get moving.

The first time you do this, it would be quite jarring. However, the more you imagine the scenario and play it in your head, the better you will be at coping. Eventually you wouldn't even flinch when you think about it.

## 19. Exposure and Response Prevention.

This particular CBT technique is known to work great for people who have OCD. Put simply, it is a type of therapy that gets the client to face their fears—then try their best to keep from ritualizing. First off, note that this can be extremely anxiety provoking. This reaction is only normal, even expected during the initial stages of the therapy. Eventually, it lessens and with continued exposure, it even disappears.

For example, a friend of mine in high school had issues with germs. She would always wash or sanitize her hands, to the point where the skin on it becomes dry and flaky. When we got into college, she began taking steps to expose herself more to what she feared most.

How? We would often go on hikes where she would need to touch the ground or the plants with her bare hands. In some cases, we even walked barefoot. At first, it was very hard for her—to the point where we had to turn back because she began feeling sick. She was diligent with it, however, and today, she can do just about anything without ritualizing.

The thing with ERP, and I noticed this with my friend too, is that it does take a while and the process can be daunting. There is also some degree of stress associated with it, and I remember having to comfort her each time she felt as if she was failing at it. The important thing to keep in mind is that there's no such thing as failure—as long as you keep pushing forward in trying to break your thought pattern, you are succeeding.

## 20.   Interoceptive Exposure.

This technique is commonly used to treat panic disorder. It involves carrying out exercises that trigger the physical sensations associated with panic attacks. This includes: hyperventilation and high muscle tension. The goal here is to eliminate the conditioned response that a person has; after all, most people who have the panic disorder believe that experiencing this sensations will eventually lead to an attack.

But is that really the case? Not always.

The idea here is that in removing the fear of the stimulus associated with panic attacks, it lessens the overall instances where they do experience attacks. It seeks to get rid of the "fear of the fear" because there are cases wherein panic attacks occur simply because the individual "felt" like it was about to happen. This leads to them hyperventilating which then triggers the disorder.

For example, an individual has a fear of public speaking. In an engagement or an event, they were requested to provide a speech. Now, because of the anxiety over this task, they might begin to hyperventilate and as this happens, they also believe that a panic attack is sure to follow. However, the reality is that they only need to practice breathing exercises in order to calm down their breathing.

Now, if they use this technique, they can effectively extinguish that "fear". The fear of their hyperventilation leading to something worse. It takes practice, much like the other techniques, and it can be equally as jarring as these sensations are never pleasant. However, as we've been emphasizing since chapter 1, the more you familiarize yourself with the feeling, the less power it has over you.

The same applies here.

## 21. Progressive Muscle Relaxation (PMR).

This is a technique that's not specific to CBT, but is often used for it nevertheless. PMR is basically an exercise wherein you relax one muscle group at a time as a means of relaxing the entire body. The most ideal way to accomplish this would be to follow a guided tutorial. There are plenty of PMR audio recordings available online, but there are also therapists who offer one on one sessions for this technique.

It is a bit similar to meditation in that you'll need to be relaxed and clear-minded, but the overall experience is plenty different.

Along with this exercise, it is also recommended that you try relaxed breathing. With regular practice, you can begin to learn how to slow down your breath. You may not think much of it, but this can have a significant effect on your body.

To close this, allow us to leave you with one very important advice if you're starting CBT. Always leave yourself room to make mistakes. It will teach you a lot and help you grow. Not everyone would get these techniques on the first try, not even on the second or third. For some, it might even take years.

Remember that speed shouldn't be your biggest concern. Always work at your own pace and think about what's best for you.

# CONCLUSION

Thank you again for purchasing this book!

I hope this book was able to help you utilize effective techniques on how to overcome depression, anxiety, and phobias.

The next step is to apply what you have learned from this book and start living your life the way you want to.

Once again, don't forget to grab a copy of your Free Bonus book *"How to Talk to Anyone: 50 Best Tips and Tricks to Build Instant Rapport"*. If you want to increase your influence and become more effective in your conversations then this book is for you.

Just go to
http://ryanjames.successpublishing.club/freebonus/

Thank you and good luck!

# Thank you!

Before you go, I just wanted to say thank you for purchasing my book.

You could have picked from dozens of other books on the same topic but you took a chance and chose this one.

So, a HUGE thanks to you for getting this book and for reading all the way to the end.

Now I wanted to ask you for a small favor. **Could you please take just a few minutes to leave a review for this book on Amazon?**

This feedback will help me continue to write the type of books that will help you get the results you want. So if you enjoyed it, please let me know! (-: